My Very Own

MOTHER'S DAY

A Book of Cooking and Crafts

My Very Own
MOTHER'S DAY

A Book of
Cooking and Crafts

by Robin West

photographs by Robert L. and Diane Wolfe
illustrations by Jackie Urbanovic

Carolrhoda Books, Inc./Minneapolis

To Shotsy and Ceil and Elise

Carolrhoda Books, Inc. c/o The Lerner Group
241 First Avenue North, Minneapolis, MN 55401

Library of Congress Cataloging-in-Publication Data

West, Robin.
   My very own Mother's Day : a book of cooking and
crafts / by Robin West.
      p.   cm. — (My very own holiday books)
   Summary: Provides suggestions for celebrating
Mother's Day through recipes and instructions for
various crafts.
   ISBN 0-87614-981-6
   1. Holiday cookery—Juvenile literature. 2. Holiday
decorations—Juvenile literature. 3. Mother's Day—
Juvenile literature. 4. Handicraft—Juvenile literature.
[1. Mother's Day. 2. Cookery. 3. Handicraft.] I. Title. II.
Series: West, Robin. My very own holiday books.
TX739.W473   1996
641.5'68—dc20
                                        95-22625
                                           CIP
                                            AC

Manufactured in the United States of America
1 2 3 4 5 6 – H – 01 00 99 98 97 96

Contents

My Very Own MOTHER'S DAY

Mother's Day Greetings

Flowers, hugs, and breakfast in bed are just a few of the treats that moms like to get on Mother's Day. The calendar may say that Mother's Day happens only once a year—the second Sunday in May—but don't let that stop you from treating your mom like a queen all year round.

You don't have to wait until May to find ways to show your mom how special she is. Getting ready to celebrate Mother's Day can be almost as much fun as the holiday itself. Try your hand at fixing a bouquet of fancy paper flowers for Mom. Or ask an adult to help you whip up a tray of breakfast treats to greet your mom on her most special day.

The ideas are endless, so you'd better get started. Mother's Day will be here before you know it!

Make It Your Very Own:
How to Use This Book

RECIPES

The recipes in this book are divided into five menus, but you don't have to make a whole meal. If you are a new cook, start slowly. Choose a recipe that sounds good to you and try it. You may need lots of help in the beginning, but be patient. The more you practice, the better you'll be.

Here are some of the easier recipes to get you started:

Kupid Kabobs
Fruity Bagelettes
Dirty but Delicious Shake
Cheese Pleasin' Apples

Once you know what you're doing, it's time to make a whole meal. Try one of the menus or put together your own combination.

Here are some things to consider when planning a menu:

Nutrition: Balance your menu by preparing plenty of fruit dishes, vegetables, and grains, along with smaller amounts of dairy products, meats, and other proteins. You can fill out your menu with foods that don't need recipes, such as bread, fresh fruits, raw vegetables, milk, and cheese.

Variety: Include different tastes and textures in your meal. If one food is soft and creamy, serve it with something crunchy. Salty foods taste good when served with something sweet. Try to include a variety of colors so the food is as pretty to look at as it is good to eat.

Theme: Each of the menus in this book has a theme, just to make it more fun. Try to think up a theme of your own and choose recipes that go with it. How about a menu of all the foods that your mom likes best? Why not serve an all-fruit snack, including Cran-Apple Salad, Fruity Bagelettes, and Strawberries Supreme? Or forget about planning a meal and make a variety of desserts instead. Anything is possible!

Be sure to share your masterpiece with someone else. Whether you make one dish or an entire meal, half the fun of cooking is watching someone else enjoy the food.

CRAFTS

Like the recipes, all the crafts in this book are easy to make, but some are easier than others. If you haven't tried making crafts before, start with something easy, like a Helping-Hands Recipe Holder or some Fancy Flowers. As you gain confidence, put together some Oodles-of-Noodles Jewelry or an Easy-Reading Book Weight. Once you've tackled these crafts, you'll be ready to make a Basket of Love.

Use your imagination when decorating your crafts. Markers, colored construction paper, scraps of fabric, and glitter will give your craft a personal touch.

Cooking Smart

Whether you are a new or experienced cook, these cooking tips can help you avoid a kitchen disaster.

BEFORE YOU COOK

- Get yourself ready. If you have long hair, tie it back to keep it out of the food, away from flames, and out of your way. Roll up your sleeves and put on an apron. Be sure to wash your hands well with soap.
- Read through the entire recipe and assemble all the ingredients. It's no fun to find out halfway through a recipe that you're out of eggs.
- Go through the recipe with an adult helper and decide which steps you can perform yourself and which you'll need help with.

WHILE YOU COOK

- Raw meat and raw eggs can contain dangerous bacteria. After handling these raw foods, wash your hands and any utensils or cutting boards you've used. Never put cooked meat back on an unwashed plate that has held raw meat. Any dough that contains raw eggs isn't safe to eat until it is cooked.
- Keep cold foods in the refrigerator until you need them.
- Wash fruits and vegetables thoroughly before using them.
- Turn pot handles to the back of the stove so the pots won't be knocked off by accident. When you are taking the lid off a hot pan, always keep the opening away from your face so the steam won't burn you.

- Use a pot holder when handling hot pans. Be sure the pot holder is dry before you use it. Heat from a pan will come right through a wet pot holder.
- Always turn off the stove or oven as soon as you're done with it.
- Be careful with foods when they come out of the microwave. Although the food may seem to be cool to the touch, microwaving can produce hot spots. When you're heating a liquid in the microwave, stir it often to distribute the heat evenly.
- Only use microwave-safe dishes in the microwave. Never put anything metal in the microwave.
- Don't cut food in your hand. Use a cutting board.
- Carry knives point down.
- Be careful when opening cans. The edges of the lids are very sharp.
- Try to clean up as you go along.

AFTER YOU COOK
- Once you've finished cooking, be sure to store your creation in the refrigerator if it contains any ingredients that might spoil.
- Be a courteous cook: clean up your mess. Leave the kitchen looking as clean as (or cleaner than) you found it.

SOME CRAFTY TIPS
Assembling a craft is a lot like cooking, and many of the same tips apply. Read the instructions and gather your supplies before you start. Play it safe with your supplies, especially scissors, and be sure to get an adult friend to help you when you need it. Put down newspapers to protect your work surface. And, of course, be sure to clean up your mess when you're done.

Good Morning Breakfast

Hidden Treasure Hearts

▼

Kupid Kabobs

▼

Hot Maple Moo

▼

Oodles-of-Noodles Jewelry

Hidden Treasure Hearts

YOU WILL NEED:

4 slices whole wheat bread

¼ cup crunchy peanut butter

1 tablespoon raisins

2 teaspoons butter, softened at room temperature

SPECIAL EQUIPMENT: heart cookie cutter

❶ Place bread slices on a cutting board. Use cookie cutter to cut heart shapes out of each slice. Depending on the size of your cookie cutter, you will be able to cut 4 to 8 hearts out of the bread.

❷ Combine peanut butter and raisins in a small bowl. Spread equal amounts of mixture on half of the heart shapes. Top each covered piece with a heart-shaped bread slice.

❸ Spread butter evenly on both sides of sandwiches.

❹ Place sandwiches in a skillet and cook over low heat. Turn to brown on each side. Serve warm.

Serves 2

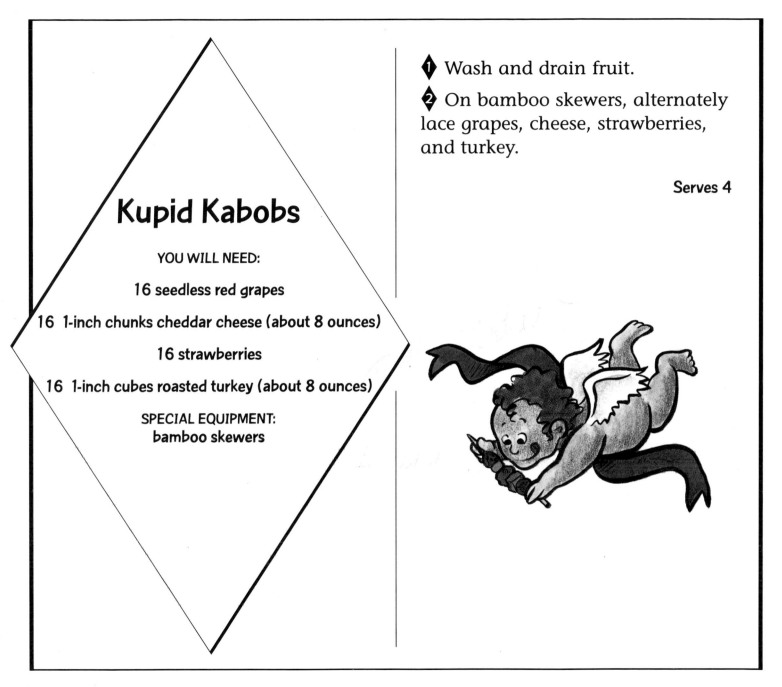

Kupid Kabobs

YOU WILL NEED:

16 seedless red grapes

16 1-inch chunks cheddar cheese (about 8 ounces)

16 strawberries

16 1-inch cubes roasted turkey (about 8 ounces)

SPECIAL EQUIPMENT:
bamboo skewers

❶ Wash and drain fruit.

❷ On bamboo skewers, alternately lace grapes, cheese, strawberries, and turkey.

Serves 4

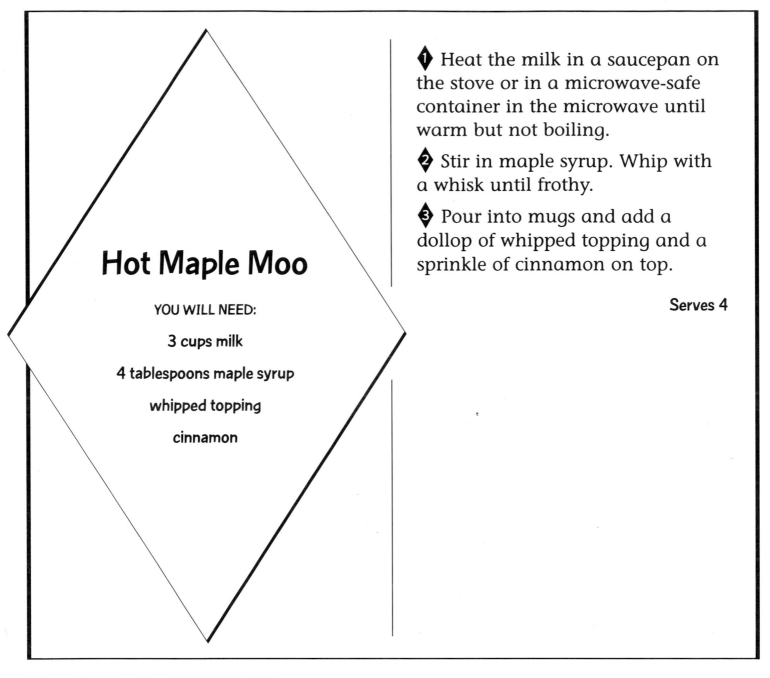

Hot Maple Moo

YOU WILL NEED:

3 cups milk

4 tablespoons maple syrup

whipped topping

cinnamon

❶ Heat the milk in a saucepan on the stove or in a microwave-safe container in the microwave until warm but not boiling.

❷ Stir in maple syrup. Whip with a whisk until frothy.

❸ Pour into mugs and add a dollop of whipped topping and a sprinkle of cinnamon on top.

Serves 4

The First Mother's Day

Your mother's favorite holiday got its start with one daughter and her very special mother. Miss Anna Jarvis of Philadelphia, Pennsylvania, thought that the country needed a day especially for mothers. Her own mother, Mrs. Anna Reeves Jarvis, had been very special to young Miss Anna and to many others in the town where she had lived.

In the past, other people had tried to start a holiday honoring all mothers, but the idea had never caught on. Anna decided that a celebration for her own mother was a good way to begin. Two years after her mother died, Anna planned to honor her mother with a Mother's Day. One Mother's Day celebration was in Philadelphia where Anna lived, and the other was in Grafton, West Virginia, where her mother had left behind many friends. At the church in Grafton, Anna gave out carnations, her mother's favorite flower.

Those first Mother's Day celebrations took place on May 10, 1908. Just a year later, many churches and Sunday Schools across the country started honoring mothers with services and carnations. People thought it was such a good idea that in 1914 the United States Congress made Mother's Day an official American holiday. Now every one celebrates on the second Sunday in May.

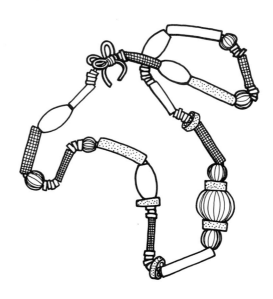

Oodles-of-Noodles Jewelry

YOU WILL NEED:

rubbing alcohol

food coloring

uncooked pasta (rigatoni, wheels, hearts, rings, etc.)

unvarnished wooden beads

thin plastic cording

❶ To make each dye color, ask an adult to help you mix 1 cup of rubbing alcohol with several drops food coloring in a bowl. Add uncooked pasta and wooden beads to the mixture and stir gently. Allow pasta and beads to remain in the mixture until the desired color is reached. Drain and spread the pasta and beads on paper towel to dry.

❷ Place your pasta and beads on a flat surface in the order in which you want them to be on your jewelry. Cut a length of plastic cording slightly longer than you want the jewelry to be.

Note: Can you think of other things to string onto your jewelry? Buttons, shells, and glass or plastic beads will make necklaces and bracelets extra special. Use your imagination to make your creations unique!

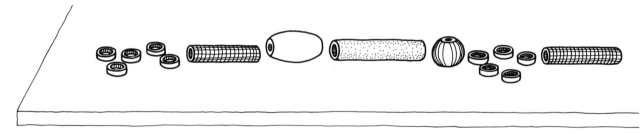

❸ String the pasta and beads onto the cording and tie ends together securely in a bow or a square knot.

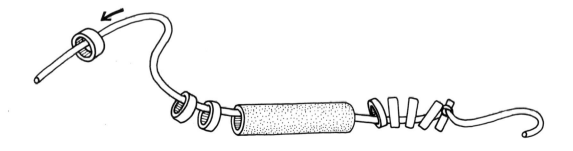

Spring Breeze Brunch

Delights of the Garden Quiche

▼

Fruity Bagelettes

▼

Mocha Cooler

▼

Strawberries Supreme

▼

Basket of Love

To: MOM
WITH LOVE

Delights of the Garden Quiche

YOU WILL NEED:

4 hard-boiled eggs

1 15-ounce can asparagus spears

1 medium zucchini, chopped

1 small tomato, cored and chopped

$\frac{1}{4}$ cup grated Parmesan cheese

1 cup milk

2 eggs

$\frac{1}{2}$ cup all-purpose baking mix, such as Bisquick

$\frac{1}{2}$ teaspoon salt

$\frac{1}{2}$ teaspoon dill weed

$\frac{1}{4}$ teaspoon pepper

❶ Preheat oven to 400°. Grease a 10-inch pie plate.

❷ Peel eggs and slice in half. In the bottom of the pie plate, arrange egg slices. Drain asparagus spears and add in a spoke pattern. Top with chopped zucchini and tomato. Sprinkle with cheese.

❸ In a medium bowl, beat milk, eggs, baking mix, salt, dill weed, and pepper. Use a whisk and beat well to avoid lumps. Pour mixture into pie plate.

❹ Bake for 25 minutes or until a knife inserted in the center comes out clean. Let stand 5 minutes before cutting. Serve warm.

Serves 4 to 6

Fruity Bagelettes

YOU WILL NEED:

1 8-ounce package cream cheese, softened at room temperature

$\frac{1}{2}$ cup strawberry preserves

$\frac{1}{2}$ teaspoon almond extract

12 frozen mini bagels, thawed and toasted

3 tablespoons toasted, sliced almonds

◆ Combine cream cheese, preserves, and almond extract in a bowl.

② Spread cream cheese mixture onto bagelettes with a knife.

❸ Sprinkle with toasted almonds and serve.

Serves 4 to 6

Kind Words for Mom

Mother's Day is a great time to express yourself and to let your mom know how much you appreciate her. To do both at the same time, grab a pencil and a piece of paper or sit down at a computer and start writing!

Your mother is sure to want to read your essay on 'The Greatest Thing My Mother Ever Did for Me.' You could put down on paper the story of how she sat in the rain to watch your soccer team win a game. Or you could describe the time when you were sick and she picked you up at school. Whatever topic you choose, write carefully and neatly. Ask a friend or teacher to read your essay to help you find ways to improve it.

If essays aren't your style, make a poster to honor 'The Best Mom in the World.'

What is it about your mom that makes her so special? Make a list of her finest qualities, the things you like best about her. Once you know what you want to say, draw your mother's picture on a large piece of paper. Surround the picture with words and phrases from your list.

Making a coupon booklet is another way to be creative and give your mom a great gift. First think of all the different things you can do to help your mom. Then make a one-page coupon for each one. Your coupons might be 'Good for one hug' or 'Good for taking out one sack of trash.' Once you have a handful, staple the coupons together along one edge. Your mother can tear them out as needed.

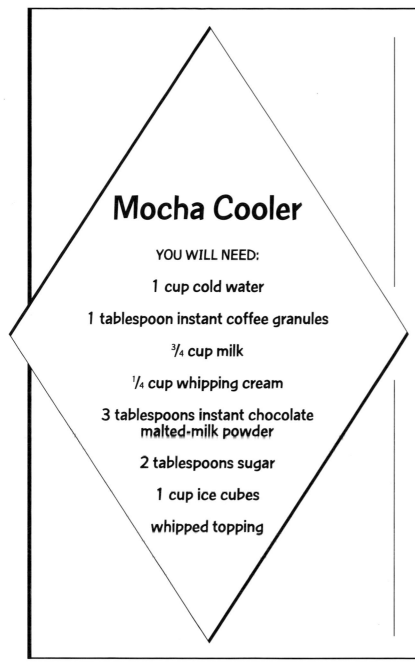

Mocha Cooler

YOU WILL NEED:

1 cup cold water

1 tablespoon instant coffee granules

¾ cup milk

¼ cup whipping cream

3 tablespoons instant chocolate malted-milk powder

2 tablespoons sugar

1 cup ice cubes

whipped topping

❶ In a blender, combine water, coffee granules, milk, whipping cream, malted-milk powder, and sugar. Blend until smooth.

❷ Add ice cubes. Cover and blend until ice is crushed.

❸ Pour into glasses and top with a dollop of whipped cream. Serve immediately.

Serves 4

Strawberries Supreme

YOU WILL NEED:

1 6-ounce package
strawberry gelatin

1 cup finely ground pecans

1 cup finely shredded coconut

¾ cup sweetened condensed milk

½ teaspoon vanilla extract

SPECIAL EQUIPMENT:
green food coloring

toothpicks

tracing paper

green construction
paper

1 In a large bowl, mix together gelatin, pecans, coconut, condensed milk, and vanilla.

2 With clean hands, shape heaping tablespoons of the mixture into strawberry shapes.

3 Place on a cookie sheet, cover with plastic wrap, and place in the refrigerator to chill for at least 1 hour.

4 While strawberries are chilling, bring 1 cup water to a boil. Pour into a shallow bowl and add several drops green food coloring. Drop toothpicks into the green water to dye them green. Dry the dyed toothpicks on paper towels.

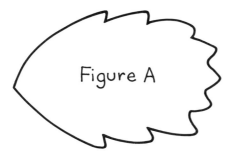

Figure A

5 Place tracing paper on figure A, the strawberry leaf pattern, above. Draw the pattern onto tracing paper and cut out the leaf shape. Place the shape over construction paper, draw around the shape in pencil, and cut out 30 green paper leaves.

6 To assemble, punch a toothpick through the center of a paper leaf. Remove chilled strawberries from refrigerator and insert a toothpick and leaf into each strawberry shape.

Makes 30

Just for Mom

If you can't think of anything to do for your mom, don't worry. Here are some great ideas to make her day extra special:

◆ Make a special T-shirt for Mom. First, buy a plain T-shirt (in your mom's size, of course). Take fabric markers or paints and draw a Mother's Day message or picture on it. Make sure you let the T-shirt dry before you give it to Mom.

◆ Take your mom to a greenhouse and buy a plant for her. Then offer to plant it with her.

◆ Write a Mother's Day song and sing it for your mom.

◆ Wash your mom's car, if she has one.

Basket of Love

YOU WILL NEED:

ruler

scissors

3 yards paper twist
(found at craft and fabric stores)

1 plastic fruit basket

2 feet ribbon (1 inch wide)

clear-drying glue (look
for Super Tacky in
fabric and
craft stores)

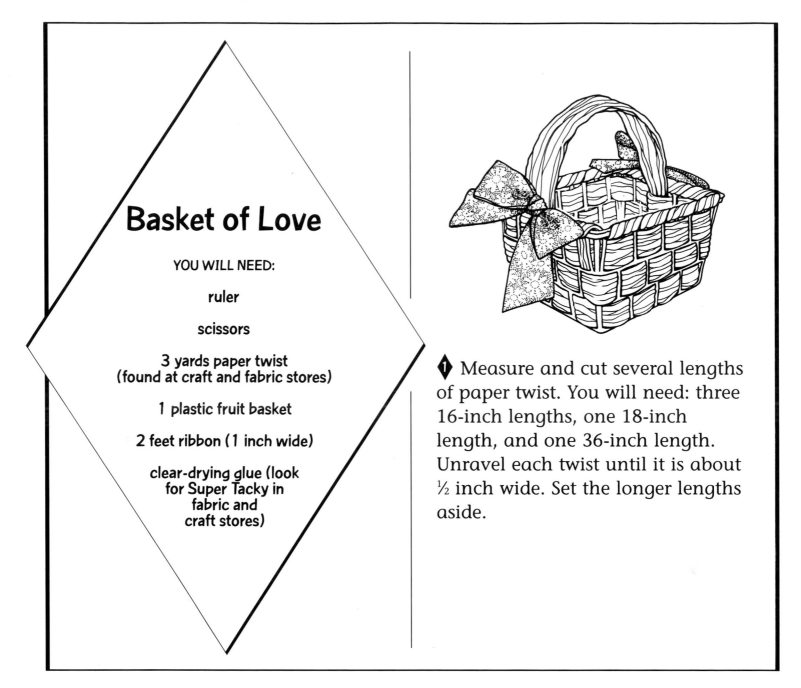

1 Measure and cut several lengths of paper twist. You will need: three 16-inch lengths, one 18-inch length, and one 36-inch length. Unravel each twist until it is about ½ inch wide. Set the longer lengths aside.

2 Take one of the 16-inch lengths and fold it in half to find its midpoint. Weave the paper in and out of the top row of the plastic grid so that the midpoint wraps around the plastic grid as shown.

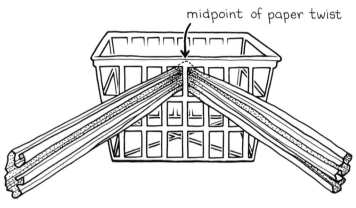

midpoint of paper twist

3 Lead paper ends in and out through the top row of the grid until completely woven. Overlap ends and tuck inside plastic grid.

4 Use the other 16-inch lengths to weave through the middle and bottom rows of the plastic basket. Begin weaving at a point to the right or left of the starting point of the row above.

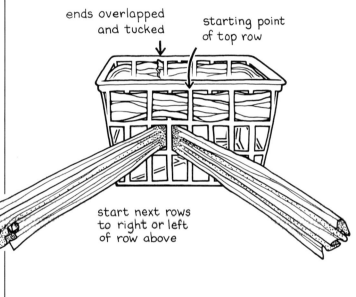

ends overlapped and tucked

starting point of top row

start next rows to right or left of row above

⬥5 Take the longest length of paper twist and fold it in half to find the midpoint. Weave the paper in and out of the top of the plastic grid so that the midpoint wraps around the very top edge of the basket. Lead paper ends in and out through the grid until completely woven. Tuck ends inside the basket. Trim excess paper if necessary.

⬥6 Use the last paper length to make the basket's handle. Insert one end into the basket, weaving it through the paper in the top row. Pull the paper end through until it meets the opposite edge of the basket. Unravel the end of the paper twist completely to cover the basket's bottom. Repeat with the other end, weaving it into the other side of the basket and unraveling the paper end.

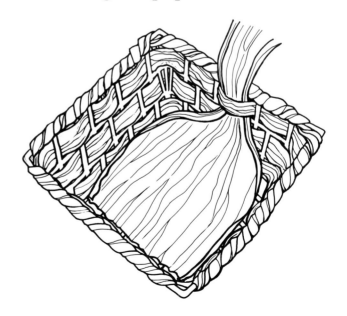

◆ Cut the ribbon into two 12-inch lengths. Tie each length into a bow. Use scissors to trim the ends if necessary. Using strong, clear-drying glue, attach a bow to either side of the basket as shown.

Note: Fill your basket with something that shows your mom how much you care. If you are filling the basket with food, be sure to line it first with a pretty napkin. If you want to fill the basket with fresh flowers, clean out an empty margarine tub or tuna can. Place the tub or can in the basket, fill it with water, and add your flower arrangement.

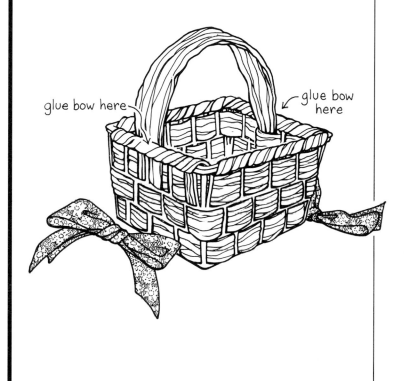

glue bow here

glue bow here

Picnic
in Paradise

Petuna Swirls

▼

Eggstraordinary Bugs

▼

Rolling Stones Salad

▼

Dirty but Delicious Shake

▼

Ants Go Marching Cookies

▼

Fancy Flowers

Petuna Swirls

YOU WILL NEED:

1 6½-ounce can tuna,
packed in water, drained

2 tablespoons mayonnaise

2 tablespoons green onion, chopped

1 tablespoon pickle relish

¼ teaspoon fresh lemon juice

4 slices whole wheat or pumpernickel bread

butter

carrots, cut into thin slices or curls

fresh chives

SPECIAL EQUIPMENT:
rolling pin

❶ In a large bowl, combine tuna, mayonnaise, onion, pickle relish, and lemon juice. Blend to a fine mixture.

❷ Cut the crusts off the bread and flatten each with a rolling pin until the bread is ⅛ inch thick. Be careful not to tear the bread.

❸ Spread a thin layer of tuna on each slice. Lay the slices on a slightly damp cloth and roll up each of them as you would a jelly roll. Seal the seam with a dab of butter.

❹ Cut each roll into three equal sections. Arrange them swirl side up surrounded by carrot petals and chive stems.

Serves 4

Eggstraordinary Bugs

YOU WILL NEED:

8 hard-boiled eggs

¼ cup finely chopped
red pepper

¼ cup mayonnaise

1 teaspoon dried onion flakes

1 teaspoon spicy mustard

⅛ teaspoon salt

¼ teaspoon pepper

16 jumbo pasta shells

pretzel sticks

stuffed green olives

Italian dressing (optional)

SPECIAL EQUIPMENT:
toothpicks

❶ Peel and chop eggs. In a large bowl, combine eggs, red pepper, mayonnaise, onion flakes, mustard, salt, and pepper. Blend well.

❷ Cook pasta shells according to package instructions, drain, and cool. Fill pasta shells with 1 heaping tablespoon of egg mixture.

❸ Arrange shells on a plate, placing the open side of the shell down.

❹ Decorate by tucking pretzel sticks under the shell shapes to form legs. Spear olives with toothpicks and insert 2 into each shell to form eyes.

❺ Drizzle dressing over bugs if desired.

Serves 4

Rolling Stones Salad

YOU WILL NEED:

1 15-ounce can kidney beans

1 15-ounce can garbanzo beans

2 or 3 pickled jalapeño peppers

8 thin slices salami, cut into strips

½ cup grated cheddar cheese

1 3½-ounce can whole black olives, drained

DRESSING:
¼ cup bottled Italian dressing

2 tablespoons lemon juice

1 small onion, minced

¼ cup fresh parsley, minced

black pepper

❶ Rinse and drain beans. Slice jalapeño peppers, being sure to remove seeds.

❷ In a large salad bowl, combine beans, jalapeño peppers, salami, cheese, and olives. Toss to mix well. Cover and refrigerate until ready to serve.

❸ In a smaller bowl, combine dressing, lemon juice, onion, and parsley. Add black pepper to taste. Stir well. Cover and refrigerate until ready to serve.

❹ To serve, place salad in individual bowls or plates and add dressing to taste.

Serves 6

Dirty but Delicious Shake

YOU WILL NEED:

8 cream-filled chocolate sandwich
cookies, such as Oreos

2 tablespoons malted-milk powder

1 ½ cups milk

4 scoops vanilla ice cream

❶ In a blender, crush cookies into crumbs. Reserve 1 tablespoon.

❷ Add malted-milk powder, milk, and ice cream to blender and blend until smooth.

❸ Pour into 4 glasses and sprinkle with reserved cookie crumbs. Top each with another cookie if desired. Serve immediately or freeze first and take along to your picnic.

Makes 4

Ants Go Marching Cookies

YOU WILL NEED:

15 graham crackers

1 cup (2 sticks) butter or margarine

1 cup firmly packed brown sugar

1 teaspoon vanilla extract

1 ⅓ cups chopped pecans

1 cup semisweet miniature chocolate chips

1 cup raisins

1 Preheat oven to 350°. Grease a large cookie sheet. Arrange crackers side by side, edges touching, on the sheet.

2 Melt butter in a microwave-safe glass bowl in a microwave oven.

3 Add sugar to melted mixture and microwave for 1 minute. Stir until sugar is completely dissolved. Add vanilla and microwave 1 minute more, or until the mixture is the consistency of soft caramel.

4 Pour the caramel mixture over the crackers. Sprinkle with chopped pecans.

5 Bake for about 10 minutes, until topping turns brown and bubbly.

⑥ Remove from oven and immediately sprinkle with chocolate chips and raisins. Cool for 5 minutes on cookie sheet, then cut into squares and separate. Transfer cookies to a cooling rack to cool completely.

Makes 30

Picnics, Indoors and Out

Moms like picnics, especially when they don't have to plan them. When picnicking outdoors, don't forget to bring some important items. You will need paper plates, paper cups, forks, knives, and spoons. Also, you'll probably want to bring napkins and a rag in case anything spills. Salt, pepper, mayonnaise, mustard, and ketchup are always nice to have, too.

Consider putting food in plastic bowls with lids to protect them from bad weather or pesky ants. For safety, don't leave mayonnaise or foods containing uncooked eggs in the sun. If they get hot, they may make you ill.

If the weather isn't nice, try picnicking indoors. For fun, make a big bright sun to hang up on the wall. Use a picnic basket, paper plates, and plastic forks and spoons, so you'll feel like you're outside. And if you have any toy ants or bugs, bring them along, too!

Fancy Flowers

YOU WILL NEED:

extra-long green pipe cleaners

buttons and beads

scissors

**paper twist (found at craft and fabric stores)
in assorted colors**

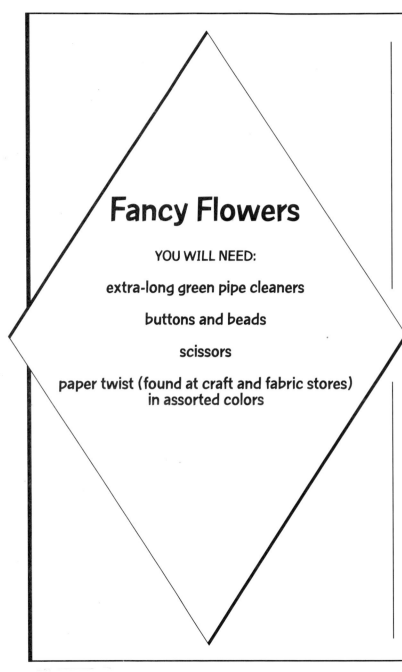

❶ For each flower, bend a pipe cleaner in half to find the midpoint. Thread a button or bead onto the pipe cleaner and carry it to the midpoint. This will form the center of your flower. Set aside.

❷ Cut paper twist in lengths ranging from 3 to 5 inches. Unravel the cut twists. You will need at least 2 unraveled twists of different lengths for each flower.

❸ Take the shortest paper twist and fold it in half to find its midpoint. Place it behind the bead or button forming the center of the flower. Twist the pipe cleaner tightly around the midpoint as shown to hold the paper in place.

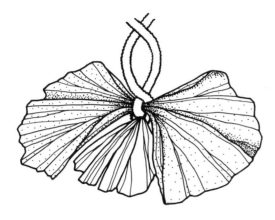

Take the next longer paper twist and repeat. Repeat again to complete your flower.

❹ To give your flower's petals a variety of shapes and textures, use scissors to round the edges or to shred or cut the twists into strips. You can fan uncut petals out wide or keep them scrunched and twisted together.

Afternoon Tea

Divine Veggie Dip
▼
Under Wraps Sausage
▼
Cheese Pleasin' Apples
▼
Crazy Crab Circles
▼
Sweetly Spiced Tea
▼
Easy-Reading Book Weight

TO: MOM WITH LOVE

Divine Veggie Dip

YOU WILL NEED:

½ cup mayonnaise

½ cup sour cream

1 teaspoon curry powder

½ teaspoon lemon juice

1 teaspoon grated onion

1 teaspoon sweet pickle relish

assorted raw vegetables to dip

❶ In a serving bowl, combine all ingredients, except for raw vegetables. Mix well. Chill until served.

❷ To serve, place bowl of dip on a platter and surround with raw vegetables cut into bite-sized pieces.

Makes 1 cup dip

Under Wraps Sausage

YOU WILL NEED:

2 cans refrigerator crescent dinner rolls
(8 rolls per can)

48 fully cooked small smoked sausage links

❶ Preheat oven to 375°.

❷ Separate dough from each can into 8 triangles. Using a kitchen knife, cut each triangle into three smaller triangles.

❸ Place sausage on short tip of dough triangle. Roll toward base of triangle, wrapping sausage in dough. Take long ends of triangle and pull toward center, pressing together firmly to seal.

❹ Place wrapped sausages 1 inch apart on ungreased cookie sheets. Bake for 12 to 15 minutes or until dough is golden brown. Serve warm.

Makes 48

Cheese Pleasin' Apples

YOU WILL NEED:

2 cups grated sharp cheddar cheese

1 1/2 ounces cream cheese

1/4 cup apple cider

1/2 teaspoon Worcestershire sauce

1/2 teaspoon dry mustard

1/8 teaspoon paprika

1 teaspoon caraway seeds

1/8 teaspoon dill weed

4 apples, cored and sliced

❶ Combine all ingredients, except for the apples, in a large bowl or in a food processor. Blend well.

❷ Transfer to a serving bowl and place on a platter surrounded by apple slices. Serve at room temperature.

Makes 1 1/2 cups dip

Crazy Crab Circles

2 8-ounce packages
cream cheese, softened
at room temperature

1/3 cup mayonnaise

2 tablespoons chopped green onion

1 teaspoon dill weed

1/4 cup chopped red pepper

1 cup shredded cheddar cheese

1 5-ounce can crab meat, drained
or
5 ounces imitation crab meat, chopped

1 package large flour tortillas

SPECIAL EQUIPMENT:
toothpicks

❶ Combine all ingredients, except for tortillas, in a large mixing bowl. Blend well.

❷ Place tortillas on a flat, clean surface and spread with a thin layer of crab mixture.

❸ Tightly roll each tortilla and cover with plastic wrap. Refrigerate at least 3 hours.

❹ To serve, remove plastic wrap, cut tortilla rolls into ¾-inch circles, spear with toothpicks, and place swirl side up on a serving platter.

Makes 64

Sweetly Spiced Tea

YOU WILL NEED:

1 cup instant orange drink, such as Tang

$1/4$ cup instant tea mix

$1/2$ cup sugar

$1/2$ teaspoon ground cloves

1 teaspoon ground cinnamon

6 cups water

whole cloves

cinnamon sticks

1 In a small bowl, combine orange drink mix, instant tea mix, sugar, ground cloves, and cinnamon. Mix well to blend.

2 Measure one third cup of drink mix and place in a large teapot. Reserve remaining mix in a jar or other clean, dry container.

3 Heat water to boiling. Pour into teapot and stir until drink mix is dissolved. To serve, pour into teacups or mugs, adding a whole clove and cinnamon stick to each cup.

Makes 6 cups tea

Note: Leftover drink mix makes a great gift for Mom. Place the mix in a clean glass jar with a lid. Decorate the jar with a length of ribbon tied in a bow.

Easy-Reading Book Weight

YOU WILL NEED:

2 metal washers
(1 ½ inches in diameter)

construction paper (red and black)

pencil

scissors

tracing paper

white liquid glue

paper punch

sequins, glitter, buttons

yarn, at least 6 inches

clear-drying glue (look
for Super Tacky in
fabric and
craft stores)

❶ Place metal washer on red construction paper. Trace around the washer onto the paper with a pencil. Cut out the circle. Trace and cut another circle from black construction paper. These will form the paper backings for the book weight. Set them aside.

❷ Place tracing paper on top of figures B, C, D, and E on page 51 and trace. Cut out tracing paper patterns.

❸ Place patterns B and C on top of red construction paper and trace around them. Be sure to trace around pattern C twice, for the ladybug's 2 wings. Cut out these construction paper figures. Repeat this step with patterns D and E, cutting them out of black construction paper.

❹ Using white liquid glue, decorate the flower-shaped construction paper figure. Attach paper, sequins, glitter, or buttons. Set aside and allow glue to dry.

❺ Glue construction paper figures C, D, and E together as shown to make a ladybug shape. Use a paper punch to make small paper circles to decorate your bug's wings.

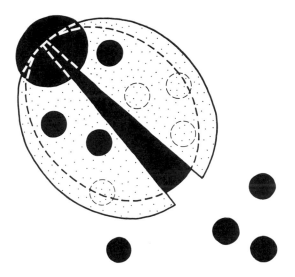

❻ Take the yarn and tie each end to a washer using a tight knot.

❼ Using strong, clear-drying glue, attach the paper circles set aside in step 1 to the backs of the washers.

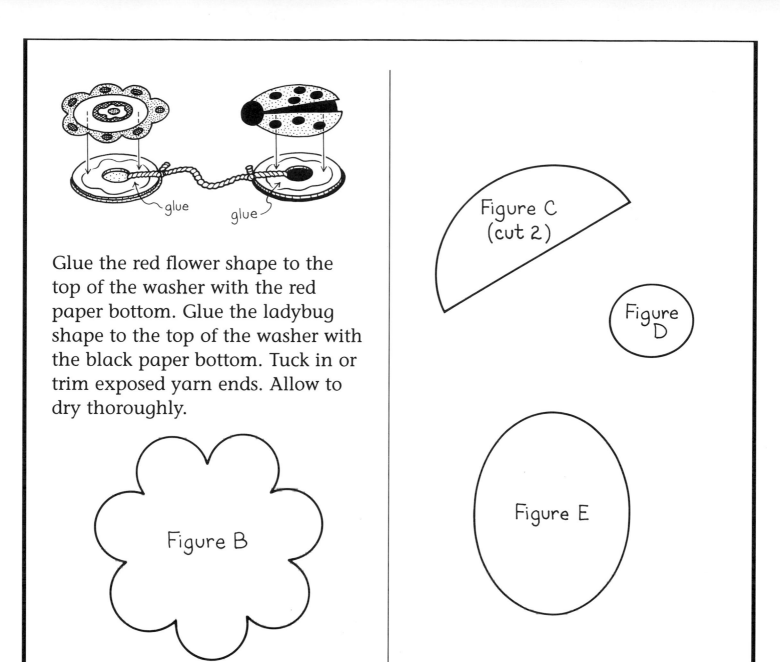

Glue the red flower shape to the top of the washer with the red paper bottom. Glue the ladybug shape to the top of the washer with the black paper bottom. Tuck in or trim exposed yarn ends. Allow to dry thoroughly.

Figure C
(cut 2)

Figure D

Figure B

Figure E

Old-Fashioned Pork Chops

You will NEED:

Serves 4

1 small can condensed golden mushroom soup
1/4 cup chopped red p...
1/4 cup chopped onion
1/4 teaspoon caraw...
1/2 teaspoon paprik...
1 1/2 cups corn br...
4 boneless pork...

TO: MOM WITH LOVE

A Down-Home Dinner

Old-Fashioned Pork Chops

▼

Peas 'n Cream

▼

Cran-Apple Salad

▼

Bundles of Joy

▼

Helping-Hands Recipe Holder

Old-Fashioned Pork Chops

YOU WILL NEED:

1 11-ounce can condensed golden mushroom soup

1/4 cup finely chopped red pepper

1/4 cup finely chopped onion

1/4 teaspoon caraway seed

1/2 teaspoon paprika

1 1/2 cups corn bread stuffing

4 boneless pork chops, 1/2 inch thick

1 tablespoon brown sugar

1 teaspoon spicy mustard

❶ Preheat oven to 400°. Lightly grease a 10-inch pie plate and set aside.

❷ In a large mixing bowl, combine soup, red pepper, onion, caraway seed, paprika, and stuffing. Spoon into pie plate.

❸ Rinse pork chops and pat dry with paper towels. Arrange pork chops over stuffing, pressing lightly into the mixture.

❹ Combine sugar and mustard in a small bowl and spread evenly over the chops.

❺ Bake for 30 minutes. Serve warm.

Serves 4

Mother's Day Puzzles

Quiz Time

Mother's Day is celebrated in many countries around the globe, and in many different ways. Match the custom with the country names below:

1. England
2. Ethiopia
3. India
4. United States

A. Treat Mom to breakfast in bed.

B. Give Mom a bunch of violets and eat a saffron-flavored cake.

C. Bring home butter, cheese, and vegetables for a special dinner.

D. Honor the mother of Mahatma Gandhi and other mothers, too.

You'll find the answers below.

1.(B) 2.(C) 3.(D) 4.(A)

Name Game

Make Mother's Day extra special by composing an acrostic based on your mother's name. An acrostic is a kind of puzzle which both spells a name or word and describes it. Here's an example:

Susan
Understands my feelings
Sends me her love when I'm away from home
Always remembers to give me a hug at night
Never makes yucky dinners.

To get started with your acrostic, write the letters of your mother's first name in a line down a page. Then think about all the things you like to do with your mom or that you like about your mom. When you've thought of several ideas, try to make them fit following one of the letters you've written down the page.

My best friend.

M
O
T
H
E
R

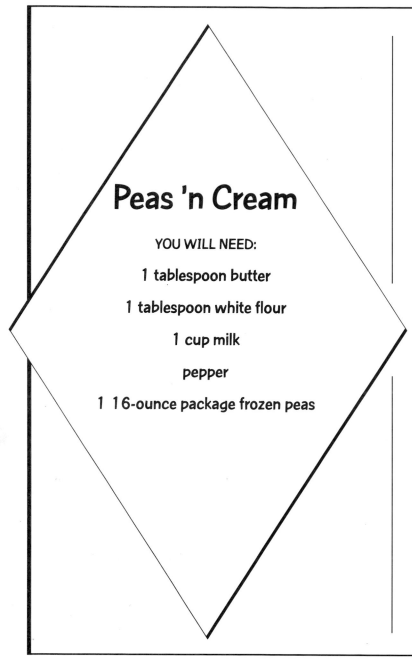

Peas 'n Cream

YOU WILL NEED:

1 tablespoon butter

1 tablespoon white flour

1 cup milk

pepper

1 16-ounce package frozen peas

❶ In a skillet, melt butter. Heat until bubbly but not browned.

❷ Add flour and stir with a fork to mix. Cook over medium heat, stirring constantly, for 2 minutes.

❸ Gradually add milk to flour and butter mixture, stirring well with a whisk to avoid lumps. Continue to heat cream sauce until it thickens. Add pepper to taste.

❹ Prepare peas according to package instructions. Ladle spoonfuls of hot cream sauce over peas and serve.

Serves 6

Cran-Apple Salad

YOU WILL NEED:

1 6-ounce package strawberry-flavored gelatin

1 ½ cups boiling water

1 16-ounce can cranberry sauce with whole cranberries

1 ½ cups apple cider

2 cups chopped apple

❶ In a large mixing bowl, empty gelatin package. Pour boiling water over gelatin and stir for 2 minutes or until gelatin is dissolved.

❷ Stir in cranberry sauce and mix well. Add apple cider and mix again.

❸ Cover bowl with plastic wrap and place in refrigerator to chill. Chill for 2 hours or until the mixture is partially set.

❹ Remove from refrigerator and add chopped apples, stirring only to mix.

❺ Pour into individual serving dishes. Cover and return to refrigerator. Chill until firm.

Serves 10

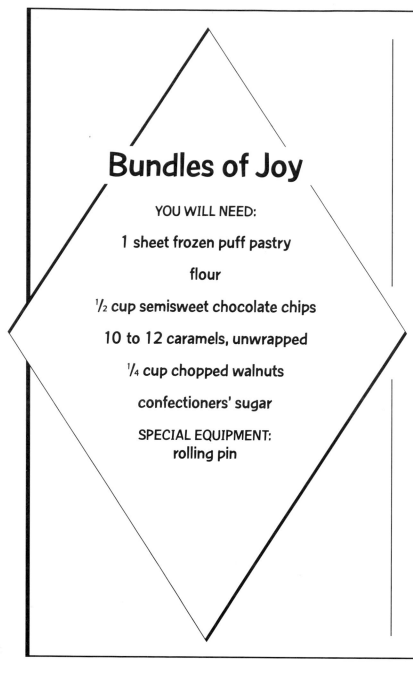

Bundles of Joy

YOU WILL NEED:

1 sheet frozen puff pastry

flour

½ cup semisweet chocolate chips

10 to 12 caramels, unwrapped

¼ cup chopped walnuts

confectioners' sugar

SPECIAL EQUIPMENT:
rolling pin

❶ Thaw pastry according to package instructions. Preheat oven to 400°.

❷ Lightly flour a flat surface. With a rolling pin, roll pastry into a 12-inch square. Lightly flour a table knife and cut the pastry into 4 equal squares.

❸ In the center of each square, place small handfuls of chocolate chips, caramels, and walnuts.

❹ With clean hands, bring the corners of each square together. Twist the ends together and turn.

❺ Place bundles twisted end up on an ungreased cookie sheet. Bake 10 to 15 minutes or until pastry is golden.

❻ Remove from oven and let stand for 10 minutes. Sprinkle with confectioners' sugar and serve warm.

Makes 4

Helping-Hands Recipe Holder

YOU WILL NEED:

pencil

colored construction paper

tracing paper (optional)

scissors

clear-drying glue (look for Super Tacky in fabric and craft stores)

clothespin

ribbon, at least 3 inches long

2 small magnets

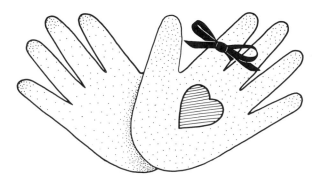

❶ To make the hands for this recipe holder, trace around your own hands onto colored construction paper or use the pattern labeled figure F on page 61. If you are using the pattern, place tracing paper on top of the figure and trace. Cut out tracing paper pattern.

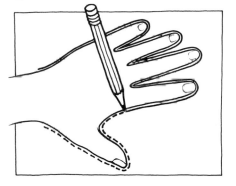

2 Place the pattern on colored construction paper and trace around it. Flip the pattern over and trace again. Cut out these construction paper hands.

3 Using clear-drying glue, attach the paper hands to either side of a clothespin as shown. Allow to dry.

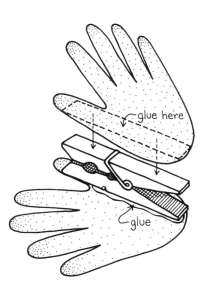

4 Decorate one of the hands with construction paper or other materials if desired. Tie the ribbon in a bow around the index finger of the paper hand. Trim ribbon ends if necessary.

5 Using clear-drying glue, attach magnets to the back of the undecorated hand as shown. Allow to dry completely before using.

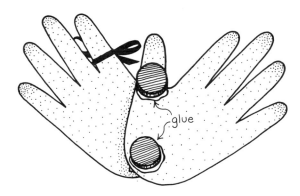

Note: Can you think of different ways to decorate your helping hands? How about adding paper fingernails, a foil ring, or even a lacy fabric cuff? Make your recipe holder special.

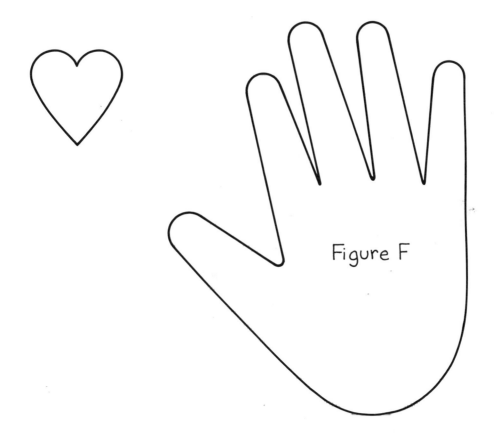

Figure F

Recipe List

Beverages
Hot Maple Moo
Mocha Cooler
Dirty but Delicious Shake
Sweetly Spiced Tea

Side Dishes and Snacks
Kupid Kabobs
Fruity Bagelettes
Eggstraordinary Bugs
Rolling Stones Salad
Divine Veggie Dip
Under Wraps Sausage
Cheese Pleasin' Apples
Crazy Crab Circles
Peas 'n Cream
Cran-Apple Salad

Main Dishes
Hidden Treasure Hearts
Delights of the Garden Quiche
Petuna Swirls
Old-Fashioned Pork Chops

Desserts
Strawberries Supreme
Ants Go Marching Cookies
Bundles of Joy

Glossary

almond extract—a liquid used to give almond flavor to food

bamboo skewer—a slender, pointed stick used to hold food in place

beat—stir rapidly

blend—use a blender to mix food together

boil—heat a liquid until it bubbles rapidly

brown—cook food, such as hamburger, until it is light brown

chill—refrigerate until cold

core—cut out the central part of a fruit, which often contains the seeds

dollop—a small amount, about a teaspoonful, of a semiliquid ingredient

drain—pour the liquid off a food

drizzle—pour a thin stream of liquid over food in a random pattern

gelatin—a clear, powdered protein substance used for thickening

grate—tear a food into small pieces by rubbing it against a grater

grease—coat with a thin layer of butter, margarine, shortening, or cooking spray

malted milk—powder prepared from dried milk and malted cereals

mince—cut into very small pieces

paprika—a red seasoning made from the ground dried pods of the capsicum pepper

pipe cleaner—a wire encased in fuzzy fabric

preheat—allow oven to heat up to a certain temperature before using

puff pastry—a pastry dough containing many alternating layers of butter and dough

rolling pin—a cylinder with handles used to roll out dough

rubbing alcohol—a cooling and soothing liquid for external application

shred—cut into long, ragged pieces

sweetened condensed milk—milk with some of the water removed and sugar added

tracing paper—paper thin enough to see through when placed on top of a pattern

vanilla extract—a liquid used to give vanilla flavor to food

whisk—a small wire kitchen tool used for beating foods by hand

Worcestershire sauce—a strong-tasting, dark brown liquid used to flavor food

Index